State of Vermont
Department of Libraries
Northeast Regional Lit
RD 2
Box 244
St. Johnsbury, VT 05819

C0-DAU-031

Discovering

SNAKES AND LIZARDS

Neil Curtis

The Bookwright Press
New York · 1986

Discovering Nature

Discovering Bees and Wasps
Discovering Snakes and Lizards
Discovering Spiders
Discovering Worms

Further titles are in preparation

All photographs from Oxford Scientific Films

First published in the United States in 1986 by
The Bookwright Press
387 Park Avenue South
New York, NY 10016

First published in 1985 by
Wayland (Publishers) Limited
61 Western Road, Hove
East Sussex BN3 1JD, England

© Copyright 1985 Wayland (Publishers) Limited

Second impression 1986

ISBN 0-531-18048-4

Library of Congress Catalog Card Number: 85-72248

Typeset by Planagraphic Typesetters Limited
Printed in Italy by G. Canale & C.S.p.A., Turin

Contents

Introducing Snakes and Lizards

Introducing Snakes and Lizards

Snakes and lizards belong to a group of animals called **reptiles.** Turtles and crocodiles are also reptiles.

People often think of reptiles as cold, slimy, wriggling creatures. But snakes and lizards are certainly not slimy and they are not usually cold, although they are often called "cold-blooded." That is because the temperature inside their body is roughly the same as that of their surroundings. So, if it is warm outside, they feel quite warm to the touch and, if it is cold, they feel rather cool.

Because they rely on the heat of the sun to warm their bodies, most reptiles

A common iguana, a kind of lizard, which lives in the trees of tropical jungles.

live in warmer parts of the world. Those living in cooler countries, such as parts of Europe, Asia and North America, **hibernate** during the winter. They will not move out from their places of shelter until warmer weather comes in spring.

Snakes and lizards have long, usually quite thin, bodies. Most lizards have four legs, which spread out sideways from their bodies, but snakes have no legs. Both lizards and snakes have tough, scaly, and nearly waterproof skins. This means that

A diamondback rattlesnake from Texas.

they can live on land without drying up. Unlike mammals, reptiles do not sweat.

Snakes and lizards breed on land. After **mating,** most snakes and lizards lay eggs. The young develop inside the eggs, which have tough, waterproof skins or shells rather like the eggs of birds. The eggs protect the young while they are growing. This has meant that reptiles have become well suited to life on land.

9

The Evolution of Snakes and Lizards

Perhaps the most famous reptiles of all were the dinosaurs. The word dinosaur means ''terrible lizard.'' They existed millions of years ago and, for a long time, they ruled the land.

There were lots of different kinds of dinosaurs. Some were big enough to be able to look over the roof of a house. Others were no bigger than a chicken. Some ate plants while others devoured the

Above *This land iguana, from the Galapagos Islands, looks a little like the dinosaurs of long ago.*

Below *Staurikosaurus, a kind of dinosaur, eating a lizard.*

contents of dinosaur eggs. We know that dinosaurs existed from their bones which have been preserved in rocks. These remains are called **fossils.**

Snakes do not look much like dinosaurs because snakes have no legs. But some lizards, like the giant Komodo dragon, look very like some dinosaurs. We know from fossils that the ancestors of dinosaurs, and of snakes and lizards, were probably the same.

Like lizards, dinosaurs laid eggs but there was an important way in which dinosaurs were different. Instead of walking with their legs splayed out on either side, dinosaurs' legs were directly under their bodies. In fact, some dinosaurs walked and ran on their hind legs only. So they were able to move quite quickly when they wanted to.

The chart below plots the evolution of reptiles and birds. It shows that lizards first appeared about 200 million years ago, and that snakes came later, about 136 million years ago.

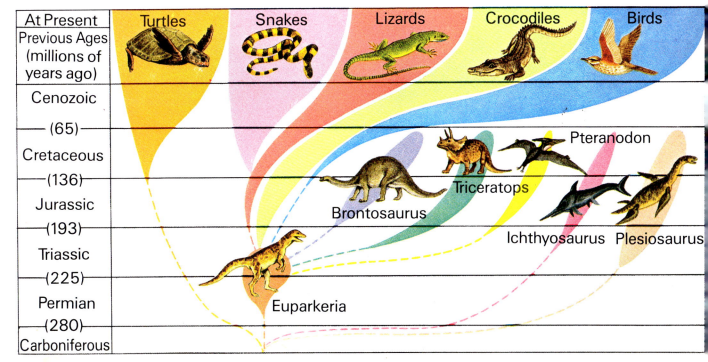

What Snakes and Lizards Look Like

What Snakes Look Like

Snakes are reptiles without legs. Some snakes may be long and thin, others short and fat. They are all roughly cylinder-shaped. The shortest snakes are about 10 cm (4 inches) long, while snakes such as pythons and anacondas may grow to more than 9 meters (30 feet) long.

Snakes, like lizards, have a scaly skin.

The **scales** on the belly of a snake help it to move. Some big snakes raise the edges of their scales and then lower them again. As they do so, this draws them forward because the free edges of their scales point backwards. Other snakes draw their bodies into a series of bends. The sides of

A Mojave rattlesnake flicking out its tongue.

their bodies press against bumps on the ground. As the bends pass backward in waves, the snake moves forwards. This works just as well in water.

The head of a snake is different from that of a lizard. There are no ear openings and the eyes do not have eyelids that can open and close. The jaw bones of most snakes are so loosely attached to each other, and to the rest of the skull, that the animal can open its mouth very wide. This means that a snake can swallow food that is bigger than its own head!

Above *The pattern of scales on each kind of snake is different. This is a close-up of a python's scales.*

The Skull of a Snake

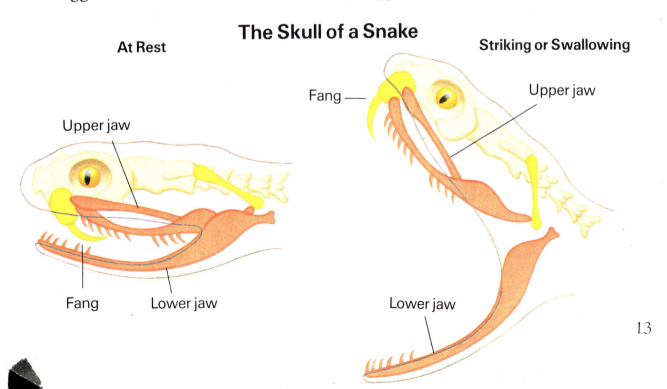

At Rest

Upper jaw

Fang   Lower jaw

Striking or Swallowing

Fang —

Upper jaw

Lower jaw

What Lizards Look Like

Lizards range in length from about 5 cm (2 inches), to as much as 3 meters (10 feet) in the case of the giant Komodo dragon. A lizard's body usually consists of a head, a trunk supported by four legs, and a tail. Lizards have rather simple teeth. Unlike snakes, lizards have ear openings on their heads and the eyes of most lizards are protected by eyelids,

You can see an ear opening and the simple teeth of this Celanese garden lizard.

A lizard's leg showing its scaly skin and a foot with five toes.

This lizard, a house gecko, has lost its tail, but it will soon grow a new one.

which they can open and close.

The tough skin of a lizard is scaly. In some lizards, there are plates of bone under the scales. Between the horny scales there is soft skin. The skin is more like a suit of chainmail than rigid armor. This means that the lizard can move its body more easily. The scales on a lizard's belly are usually bigger than those on its back. They are arranged in rows and they overlap smoothly. This scaly skin protects the lizard but it is also fairly waterproof and keeps the animal from drying up.

Many lizards have four legs. Some have very small legs and others, like the slowworms, have no legs at all. Usually, a lizard has five toes on each foot, which are often armed with claws. Different kinds of lizards can walk, run, make burrows, climb trees, swim and even glide.

The tails of many lizards break off if grasped by an enemy. It is better for the lizard to lose a tail than its life. A new tail eventually grows in place of the old one.

Where Snakes and Lizards Live

On Land

Snakes and lizards are found throughout most of the world. Many of them live in warmer regions but some snakes may be found as far north as the Arctic Circle. Most lizards and snakes live on land. They are found in all kinds of places where there is food for them to eat. Different types of snakes and lizards live in

In the rain forest of Costa Rica many snakes live on the ground, as well as climbing trees.

Above *A grass snake sheds its skin in the water. Some snakes like living near water.*

forests and woods, open grassy country, rocky hillsides, and even deserts. Some lizards are quite common on roadsides, in towns, and inside houses.

Other snakes and lizards like to live near rivers or ponds. Many can swim well and some spend a lot of time in the water. Some kinds can climb trees and there are lizards that have flaps of skin on the sides of their bodies that help them to glide through the air from tree to tree. Some tree-climbing snakes will steal the chicks from birds' nests.

With their long, thin bodies, snakes are well able to slither into cracks and crevices or even make burrows. In certain parts of the world, there are snakes that live entirely on the mud of mangrove swamps where they feed on creatures such as mudskippers, a kind of fish.

A hot desert may not seem a very good place for an animal to live. But there are snakes and lizards that survive there. Some come out at night when it is cooler, although others are active during the day. These lizards and snakes seek shade when it is very hot.

This gecko lives in the Namib desert. It digs itself into the sand to escape from enemies and from the heat of the sun.

In the Ocean

Among reptiles, it is really only the sea turtles and sea snakes that spend most or all of their lives in the ocean. The ocean is salty, and reptiles that live in salt water must be able to rid themselves of the extra salt they take in when eating and drinking. They do this through special **organs** in their bodies called salt **glands.**

There is only one kind of lizard that normally feeds in the ocean. This is the marine iguana, which is found on the rocky shores of the Galapagos Islands in the Pacific Ocean, off the west coast of

A marine iguana, from the Galapagos Islands, feeds on seaweed underwater.

This beautifully marked black and yellow sea snake is very poisonous.

South America. These remarkable creatures **bask** on the warm rocks and then dive into the cold seas to feed. They can swim well and feed on seaweed for which they dive beneath the waves. They cannot breathe underwater, and have to come up for air.

Sea snakes feed on fish and can stay underwater for long periods in search of their **prey**. They often have specially shaped bodies, which are rather flattened. The tail end may be paddle-shaped, while the head end may be much thinner than the tail end. This helps them to move quickly through the water and to strike at their prey with ease. They do not lay eggs but give birth to live young.

Food and Feeding

Finding Food

Most lizards rely mainly on their eyesight to find prey. Particularly important is a lizard's ability to notice movement.

The eyes of tree-living chameleons are rather peculiar. They are in turret-like eyeballs on each side of the animal's head. Each eye can look in different directions so that one eye can be staring backward at the same time as the other is looking forward. When one eye has spotted an insect, the chameleon then focuses on it with both eyes. If it is within range the chameleon shoots out its long, sticky tongue to capture the insect.

For some lizards, and many snakes, prey may be found by "tasting" the air. They flick out their forked tongues to pick up any scent particles carried in the air. The tongue is then drawn back and any scent particles find their way into special organs in the roof of the mouth. From these organs a message is sent to the brain which tells the snake or lizard that there may be food nearby.

Some snakes are able to find prey in complete darkness. These snakes, such as pit vipers, have special **pits** on their heads,

A rattlesnake "tastes" the air. The pit between its eye and nostril is heat sensitive.

which can detect the heat given out by warm-blooded animals, like mammals.

Hearing is probably not as important to snakes and lizards as smell and sight. Snakes do not have ear openings. They are able to feel vibrations in the ground, which may be useful for detecting prey as well as for avoiding their enemies.

A chameleon catching an insect with its long, sticky tongue. It relies on its amazing, swiveling eyes to find food.

Types of Food

Warm-blooded animals need to eat a lot of nourishing food to stay active and keep themselves warm. Cold-blooded animals, like lizards and snakes, need less energy because the sun keeps their bodies warm. Even so they must eat and reptiles feed on all kinds of different things.

Many small lizards eat insects. This gecko has caught a moth.

In the warmer parts of the world where most lizards live, there is no shortage of insects. It is hardly surprising that most lizards rely on this plentiful source of food. But it takes a lot of energy to chase and capture prey. If the only reward is a tiny insect, big lizards would soon go hungry, so they often eat mainly plants. Other large lizards may feed on animals, such as mice, frogs, small birds, or even other lizards. The poisonous gila monster attacks all kinds of creatures but also feeds

Above *Komodo dragons, the largest lizards on earth, are meat-eaters.*

Below *A small, harmless blind snake burrows into a termites' nest to feed.*

on the eggs of birds and other reptiles. The giant Komodo dragon, the largest of all living lizards, preys upon animals as big as deer and wild pigs.

The different kinds of burrowing snakes usually feed on creatures such as earthworms, ants, and termites. Sea snakes eat fish. Other snakes eat a wide range of animals including birds, eggs, bats, other mammals, slugs and snails, frogs and toads.

How Snakes Eat

All snakes have sharp, backward-pointing teeth, which they use for grabbing and holding prey, rather than for chewing.

A snake eating a frog. Snakes usually swallow their prey headfirst.

Some snakes simply stalk a victim or wait until it comes within range, then they strike forward and grab it in their jaws. As the creature struggles, the backward-pointing teeth dig in deeper and drag it farther into the snake's mouth. The live prey is then swallowed whole.

Above *A sand-snake squeezing its prey, a lizard, to death.*

Other snakes are called constrictors. These include the large pythons and boas. A constricting snake strikes at its prey and then coils its body around the animal. Each time the victim breathes out, the snake tightens its grip. Eventually, the poor creature cannot breathe at all and dies from suffocation. It is then swallowed whole, head first.

Finally, there are poisonous snakes, some of which can kill humans. These snakes have hollow or grooved fangs in the top jaw. When they strike at the prey, these fangs inject poison into the animal either to paralyze or to kill it. The poison is contained in special glands. Some poisonous snakes can spit **venom.** They usually aim accurately at the eyes so that their prey is blinded.

Below *A poisonous snake biting a lizard. The snake's venom quickly kills its prey.*

Reproduction

Courtship and Mating

For various reasons, all animals die after a certain time. They must find a way to **reproduce,** otherwise they would soon disappear or die out. Snakes and lizards, like many other animals, have males and females, which need to come together, or mate. When mating occurs, the male climbs onto the female's back and injects his **sperm** into her body to **fertilize** her eggs. A new reptile can grow from every fertilized egg.

There is often a particular time of year when snakes and lizards come together to mate. This is called the breeding season.

Two adders, a male and a female, have come together to mate.

Male

Female

Males and females must be able to recognize each other. Male and female lizards are often different colors. Some males have very bright colors and attract females by head-bobbing or knee-bending. Some have brightly colored flaps of skin on the throat, which they unfold when they are **courting.** This may drive away other males and attract females. Sometimes, two males will actually fight to compete for females and for a place where mating takes place.

Male snakes usually find a female by following her scent trail. The male then rubs his chin against the female and flicks his tongue over her body. Finally, he coils his body around hers to mate.

Above   *The more colorful of these two mating lizards is the male.*

Two iguanas from Fiji. The brightly striped male is courting the female.

27

Laying Eggs or Giving Birth

Fertilization of snakes' and lizards' eggs takes place inside the female's body. A female lizard or snake usually produces quite a small number of large eggs. The eggs have big yolks which supply nourishment for the growing young. Most females lay their eggs on the ground before they hatch. The eggs are protected by a tough skin or shell. In some cases, however, all of the development of the young reptiles takes place inside the mother's body and, instead of laying eggs, the young are born alive.

Most lizards dig some kind of nest hole in which to lay their eggs. Few snakes build nests of any kind, and the eggs are simply laid among rocks, in tunnels or burrows, or among piles of leaves. Most snakes and lizards leave their eggs after laying them. The eggs are kept warm, or **incubated,** by the heat of the

Grass snakes often lay their eggs in a manure or compost heap.

Above *The newly hatched gecko looks funny with a piece of shell on its head.*

sun. Some lizards, however, will look after their eggs to make sure they stay warm and to protect them from enemies. There is even one kind of python that coils its body around the eggs to incubate them.

When they are ready to hatch, young reptiles usually break out of the eggs using a sharp tooth called the "egg tooth," at the tip of the upper jaw. The egg tooth drops off soon after hatching.

The sharp egg tooth of this hatching python can just be seen at the tip of its nose.

From Babies to Adults

On average most eggs take several weeks to hatch, depending on the climate. Most snakes and lizards do not look after their young after they have hatched. The babies are left to fend for themselves. Some lizards, such as the great plains skink, do

An adder with its babies which are much browner than the parent.

help the young to break out of the eggs.

Most young animals tend to grow quickly at first. Then, when they have reached adulthood, the growth slows down or even stops. Lizards and snakes are no exception to this, although the larger kinds may go on growing throughout life. Males and females may be different sizes.

From time to time, snakes and lizards shed their skins to allow more room for

A garden lizard shedding its old skin to reveal a glossy new one underneath.

growth. This is called sloughing (sluffing). The first slough takes place shortly after the creature has hatched. Then it occurs regularly throughout the animal's life. A snake sheds it skin in one piece. The sloughed skin looks just like an empty snake, but the skin is inside out.

Lizards, on the other hand, shed their skins in pieces. It is possible to tell when a reptile is about to slough its skin because its appearance changes — it looks rather milky in color especially in its eyes.

From studies of reptiles that have been kept in captivity, it seems that few lizards live longer than twenty years, while snakes may reach an age of thirty. In the wild they probably do not live this long.

31

Survival in a Dangerous World

A mongoose family investigating a puff adder in Kenya, Africa.

Enemies of Snakes and Lizards

Just as lizards and snakes feed on other creatures, they themselves may also be eaten. There are many kinds of animals that eat snakes and lizards, including other snakes and lizards, and some birds and mammals.

A famous story by Rudyard Kipling describes a battle between a mongoose and a cobra. Many people think that mongooses feed mainly on poisonous snakes, but that is unlikely.

The African secretary bird specializes in killing and eating venomous snakes. It literally stamps them to death while protecting itself from their bites with its wings.

Although there are many animals that eat snakes and lizards, there is only one animal that poses a real threat to their numbers — humans. People threaten the

Above *This roadrunner has caught a lizard to offer to its mate.*

existence of snakes and lizards in many different ways. Many people are afraid of snakes, and when they come across one, they are tempted to kill it, even though it may be harmless.

One of the worst effects of human activity on the lives of snakes and lizards is the destruction of the places in which they live. People cut down forests, drain marshes and turn deserts into farm land. Some kinds of reptiles may benefit from this but most suffer because they cannot live anywhere else.

Below *When threatened, some snakes, like this grass snake, pretend to be dead.*

Deadly to Humans

There are few lizards that are poisonous, and the snakes that just grab their prey or that constrict them are no real threat to people. Even the bite of some poisonous snakes would have little effect on a reasonably healthy person. Most snakes naturally try to escape from people rather than attack.

But there are some snakes that can be deadly to people. These are vipers, cobras and sea snakes. It is worth being

A black spitting cobra ready to strike. It can spit venom at its enemies.

Camouflage

All animals eat, and many are food for other animals. For the survival of any animal, it is obviously best to avoid being eaten. One way to do this is not to be

This Texas horned lizard is wonderfully camouflaged on the ground.

seen. The creature must blend in with its background. This is called camouflage. If the color and pattern of the creature match its surroundings, it will obviously be hard to see.

Some kinds of snakes and lizards achieve this remarkably well with their greenish or brownish mottled and patched skin color. Perhaps the most amazing

careful in areas where venomous snakes are known to live because most snake bites result from accidentally bumping into one.

The venoms of snakes are of two main kinds. One type is a nerve poison. This kind of venom may affect the muscles of the heart or prevent the victim from breathing. The other type of venom affects the flesh or the blood and may cause massive internal bleeding.

It is possible to make substances called antiserums or antivenins which are used

A tiger rattlesnake being milked of its venom. The venom is used to make anti-snakebite serum.

to treat snake bites. This is done by capturing the snake and forcing it to bite into a piece of plastic covering a jar. The venom is collected in the jar and the fluid made from this is then injected into the sufferer to counteract the poison. Unfortunately, some antiserums are difficult to obtain and doctors are not able to treat all snake bites properly.

Above *This snake's mottled skin breaks up its outline, and makes it hard to see.*

camouflage artist is the chameleon. It can not only change its skin color to suit its background but can even color different parts of its body in different ways.

Another method of camouflage is to break up the outline of the animal's body. Bold stripes and blotches are most effective for this purpose. This works rather in the way that a zebra's stripes break up its outline.

Often, snakes and lizards that live on the ground are darker on their backs and paler on their sides and bellies. With the sun shining from above, such an animal is more difficult to see because its paler underside disguises the shadow cast by its body.

Below *The horsewhip snake's long, twining body helps to hide it in the trees.*

Colors for Display

Some snakes and lizards may be very brightly colored. In the case of the harmless lizards, it is usually the males that have the bright colors. These col-

Most animals learn to keep away from the brightly striped coral snake with its venomous bite.

ors are important for attracting females or warning off other males in the breeding season.

Very poisonous snakes and a few venomous lizards are often colored with bands or stripes of bright red, yellow and black, like the coral snake found in southern United States. It might seem that this would make them so easy to see that they would become targets for other

animals. But, if they are dangerous, it may be better to advertise the fact. Animals that might normally prey on reptiles seem to know that these bright colors are a warning. It is actually called warning coloration.

These bright bands and stripes may serve another purpose. Although they are easy to see out in the open, the patterns help to break up the outline of the snake

The gila monster, a poisonous lizard, lives in the southern United States and Mexico.

in its normal surroundings so that it is, in fact, harder to see.

Some harmless snakes look like other snakes that are deadly. This is called mimicry. The harmless snakes may be left alone because they are mistaken for dangerous ones.

Conservation of Snakes and Lizards

All of the different living things on Earth depend upon one another in some way for survival. Lizards and snakes may not seem very important. People might think of them as so harmful or unpleasant that they should be destroyed. But life on Earth is very complicated, and destroying a creature that may be dangerous to humans could be very harmful. The balance of nature may be upset so badly that it could not be restored.

For example, chemical poisons have been used to protect crops from insects that feed on them. But useful snakes or lizards could then feed on the poisoned insects and might be killed themselves. Reptiles are also food for other animals. If

The picture below shows a chain of creatures that feed on each other. All these animals could be affected by a farmer spraying crops with poisonous chemicals.

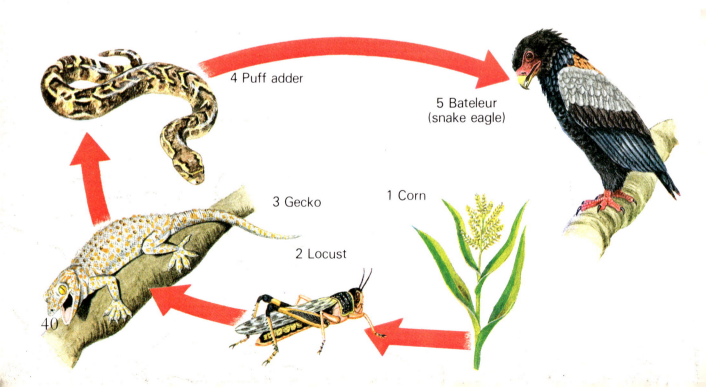

4 Puff adder

5 Bateleur
(snake eagle)

3 Gecko

1 Corn

2 Locust

the reptiles died out, so might the animals that fed on them.

We do not fully understand the delicate web of life and perhaps we never shall. Some species of reptiles have already died out, and they can never return. It is important to our own survival to protect our countryside. This includes taking care of snakes and lizards and the places where they live.

Cutting down jungles and forests destroys many of the places in which snakes and lizards live.

Studying Snakes and Lizards

In a Terrarium

You can learn a lot about snakes and lizards by reading books, going to museums, or seeing the animals in a zoo. Another way to find out more about reptiles is to keep them as pets. But remember that, even if they have been bred in captivity, they are still wild animals and must be looked after with care. It is not really a good idea to keep snakes because many need very special care and some are now becoming quite rare.

There are many lizards that you can keep, provided you give them the right kinds of conditions and food. You will need to give them a home called a terrarium. A wooden box with a glass front and a tight-fitting lid makes a good

Left *On a visit to the zoo, this little girl was able to hold a boa constrictor.*

42

terrarium. There should be air holes in the lid which can be made of wire mesh. Make sure the lid is firmly fixed to keep the animal from escaping. The size of the box depends upon the size of the lizard you are keeping. Keep your terrarium warm and dry.

Keeping any animal is a responsible job. If you just keep a small lizard, like a slowworm, you will probably be able to feed it on worms, insects, or even minced meat. It will also need fresh water every day, both for drinking and for having a bath to cool off.

Before you decide to keep a snake or a lizard, talk with other people who keep reptiles, and read books about keeping them. If your reptile is healthy, happy, and properly fed, you can learn a lot by watching its behavior. You may even be able to breed your own reptiles.

The best place to keep a snake or a lizard is in a terrarium.

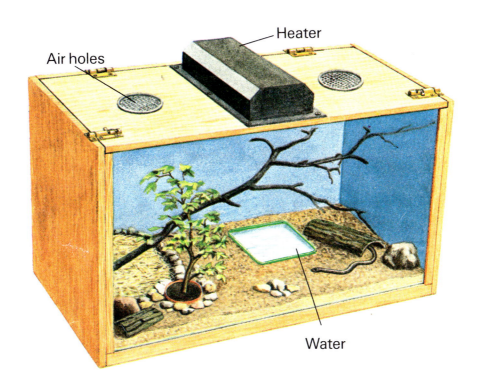

Heater

Air holes

Water

43

Out of Doors

The best way to learn about wild animals is to study them outside in their natural state. Snakes and lizards are difficult to find in the wild because they are shy and secretive. They hide away in cold, wet weather and are usually most active on warm, sunny days. Even though you do not see one, you might be able to find signs that they are around. Occasionally, you may come across the sloughed skin of a snake. You might even be able to find some reptiles in your own yard.

For example, garter snakes may

A slowworm is a lizard without legs.

be found hunting for earthworms in the garden, or looking for frogs near a pond or stream. Garter snakes are very common from Canada to Central America, especially in moist areas. If you see one, do not disturb it, for this slim little snake is quite harmless. If you stand still, you may be able to watch it hunting for food.

Never approach any snake too closely unless you are certain it is harmless. In some parts of the world, where there are more venomous reptiles, you should take extra care. Never go barefoot in places where poisonous snakes might live. It is a good idea, too, to wear long pants.

The sloughed skin of a snake.

Glossary

Bask To lie in the sun.

Courting The way in which male and female animals behave before mating occurs.

Fertilize To join together a male's sperm with a female's egg so that a new individual can grow from the fertilized egg.

Fossil Any remains or trace, such as a shell, bone, or footprint, of an animal or plant that has been preserved in rocks or mud.

Gland An organ in an animal's body, which produces substances from the blood or passes them out from the body.

Hibernate To sleep through the winter.

Incubated Eggs kept at the ideal temperature for hatching.

Mating The way in which male and female animals come together so that the female's eggs can be fertilized by the male's sperm.

Organ A part of an animal's body, such as the heart or lungs, that does a special job.

Pit Part of the double cavity that occurs in front of the eyes of some kinds of snakes. These pits are very sensitive to changes in temperature and help the snake to detect warm-blooded prey.

Prey An animal that is killed and eaten by another animal.

Reproduce To make new animals or plants of the same kind; to have offspring.

Reptile An animal, such as a lizard, snake, or turtle, which has a backbone, a scaly skin, and is cold-blooded and usually fully adapted to living on land.

Scales The small hard flakes that cover the bodies of snakes and fish.

Sperm Male sex cells, which are used to fertilize a female's eggs.

Venom The poisonous fluid, produced by some reptiles and other animals, that is injected into a victim to paralyze or kill it.

Finding Out More

If you would like to find out more about snakes and lizards, you could read the following books:

Brenner, Barbara. *A Snake-Lover's Diary.* Reading, MA: Addison-Wesley, 1970.

Chace, G. Earl. *Rattlesnakes.* New York: Dodd, Mead, 1984.

Fichter, George S. *Poisonous Snakes.* New York: Franklin Watts, 1982.

Harrison, Hal H. *World of the Snake.* New York: Harper & Row, 1971.

McClung, Robert M. *Snakes: Their Place in the Sun.* Easton, MD: Garrard Pub., 1979.

Roever, Joan M. *Snake Secrets.* New York: Walker & Co., 1979.

Simon, Seymour. *Poisonous Snakes.* New York: Four Winds/Scholastic, Inc., 1981.

Zim, Herbert S. *Snakes.* New York: Morrow.

Index

Picture Acknowledgments

Survival Anglia — J. & D. Bartlett 23 (top); J. B. Davidson 21; J. Foott 27 (top); A. Root 34; S. Trevor 32. All other photographs from Oxford Scientific Films by the following photographers: G. I. Bernard cover, opp. title page, 13, 14, 17, 24, 29 (bottom), 31, 33 (bottom), 35, 44 (top); J. A. L. Cooke 8, 9, 15 (right), 20, 23 (bottom), 29 (top), 33 (top), 36, 37; S. Dalton 15 (left); F. Ehrenstraom 25 (top); M. Fogden 25 (bottom), 38, 39; R. A. Lewin 42; Mantis Wildlife Films 27 (bottom); G. Merlen 10, 18; P. Parks 22; A. Ramage 44 (bottom); R. Redfern 30; P. K. Sharpe 16; D. Thompson 41; P. & W. Ward 19; G. J. Wren 28. Artwork by Wendy Meadway.